Pulling Down Strongholds

by John Osteen

Lakewood Church
P. O. Box 23297
Houston, Texas 77228

ISBN 0-912631-07-4

Pulling Down Strongholds

*For the weapons of our warfare are not carnal,
but mighty through God to the pulling down of strong
holds; casting down imaginations, and every high thing
that exalteth itself against the knowledge of God, and
bringing into captivity every thought to the obedience of
Christ* (2 Corinthians 10:4,5).

The message of this book is sent forth in the love
of God. It has been written because of a deep desire to
help those who are suffering defeat and do not know
how to get victory.

Even though you may have been tormented, defeated, and cast down, if you will heed the message of
this book, God will give you light on how to have
victory in your present state, and help you win every
battle in the future.

There are thousands of Christians who are going through what you are experiencing because Christians are the enemies of Satan. Satan wants to defeat Christians. He wants to deceive them. He wants to vex them. Satan wants to keep you from the Truth, for he knows that the "Truth will set you free."

The attack starts in the mind

Satan's primary attack is in the mind. He begins his battle in our thoughts. Few Christians realize this fact. They take little care in guarding their minds. They fill their minds with television programs, radio programs, newspaper articles, magazines, and the conversation of the world. Thousands of thoughts enter their minds—all concerning the things of this world.

The Bible speaks of "the weapons of our warfare"—*The weapons of our warfare are not carnal, but mighty through God to the PULLING DOWN OF STRONG HOLDS* (2 Corinthians 10:4). WARFARE! The area of our thoughts is a battlefield. The warfare starts in the mind, then spreads to other areas of our lives.

Verse 5 speaks of *CASTING DOWN IMAGINATIONS*. Wicked imaginations are from the devil. We are to PULL DOWN Satan's strongholds and CAST DOWN his thoughts, which produce wicked IMAGINATIONS.

Christians are to have the mind of Christ! David knew the secret of guarding his mind. He said, *I will set no wicked thing before mine eyes* (Psalm 101:3). He also said, *Let the words of my mouth, and the meditation of my heart, be acceptable in thy sight, O Lord* (Psalm 19:14). The meditation of our hearts—or our thought lives—should be acceptable to God. Win the battle in your mind and you will rejoice every day of your life in the victory God gives you over the enemy.

Divine visitation

Jesus said the Holy Ghost would show us things to come. In His love and mercy, He shows us things to prepare us for coming events. This has happened to me several times, and it's always a precious experience.

In 1965, the Lord gave me a very unusual visitation during the night. In this experience, the Lord showed me three different confrontations with the devil. One was a seemingly minor encounter. The next was somewhat stronger. In the last scene, I was ushered into a room where the evil genius sat—the god of this world. There was another man in that room also. He was trying desperately to get out but could not. He moved his arms and legs slowly and with great effort, trying to get to the door, but the evil one held him captive. It was a most unusual sight.

But there I was in the same room. Courage swept

5

into my heart. I said boldly, without fear or doubt, "I WILL WALK OUT OF THIS ROOM, IN THE NAME OF THE LORD JESUS CHRIST!" Upon saying that, I walked out without any difficulty at all.

Then I awoke in the middle of the night. I pondered this experience but did not fully understand the meaning until later. Little did I know that the Lord was showing me what I was to face in the next few months.

Satan's attack

Without relating it to this experience or even remembering this visitation, I suddenly felt myself being attacked by Satan. I will not describe the experience in detail, but I will tell you that, for several months, I had encounter after encounter with the enemy. It went from small battles to larger ones. Finally, I felt myself in the presence of that evil one. No words can describe the fear and torment I felt while there. God is love, but Satan is fear and torment. It was a stark reminder of how terrible it would be to be lost throughout eternity.

While in this state, feeling that I was fighting for my very life, I noticed that every time Satan attacked, it was in the area of my mind—my thought life. He assailed my mind and flooded my thoughts. He raged from every direction with thoughts that would come against me with a powerful force. It almost seemed like a physical thing.

This constant barrage of thoughts brought on a weakness in my body. I felt as though I would never be able to preach and minister again. I felt strange. The thoughts told me I had every disease in the book...that I was going to die...that I had failed God and highly displeased Him. The lying thoughts of Satan tried to convince me that this was God bringing judgment upon me for all my past sins. It was a fearful torment! I felt forsaken of God and man. This was the work of the devil!

God's counterattack

One day while in my office, I cried out to God in my suffering. I had prayed and prayed and prayed. Why did God not deliver me? In this state of mental torment and physical weakness, I asked God to help me understand.

Suddenly, He put some of HIS thoughts into my mind! I had completely forgotten about that visitation several months earlier. God reminded me of that merciful visitation. In His gentle way, He said, "My son, don't you remember that strange visitation I gave you several months ago?"

I began to think back and I said, "Yes, Lord, I do."

He said, "Tell me about it."

Then I recounted, in my silent conversation with the Lord, all the events of that visitation. When I got to the part about the third phase, where I was in the presence of the evil genius who is the god of this world, the Lord said, "My son, that is right where you are now in your experience. You have gone through the other two, and the fear and torment you feel is because you are now in that third phase. I am not tormenting you. I am not condemning you. I am not sending this fear. It is coming from the devil. I am the One who loves you. I am the One who sent my Son to die for you. I am the One who made a way for you to escape spending eternity with the devil and his angels. Hell was created for them, not for My creation."

These are some of the thoughts I had from the Lord. Then He asked me, "How did you get out of that room when the other man couldn't?"

As I sat there trembling, weak, and defeated, I suddenly realized what I had done. I said, "Lord, I stood up, filled with courage and without fear, and I boldly said, 'I WILL WALK OUT OF THIS ROOM, IN THE NAME OF THE LORD JESUS CHRIST!'"

The Lord said to me, "THEN GET UP AND DO IT!"

The victory

Praise the Lord! This was the turning point in my experience. It did not happen instantly, but through the weeks to come, I learned well my lesson from the Lord. I arose early each day and began to devour my Bible. I began to get His thoughts into my mind. I fought off the lies of Satan with the Word of God.

In my weakened state, I got a map of the world and looked at it. I boldly said, "I am going to preach the Gospel all over the world!"

The devil said, "If you get on a plane, it will fall with you."

I said, "Mr. Devil, I have some thoughts for you to think about. The Lord is going BEFORE me. The blood of Jesus is OVER me. The everlasting arms of God are UNDER me. And goodness and mercy are BEHIND me, FOLLOWING ME ALL THE DAYS OF MY LIFE!"

I pulled the sword of the Spirit every day and whipped the devil with it, in the name of Jesus of Nazareth.

When the thought came, *You are weak,* I shouted with the voice of an archangel in my spirit, "I AM STRONG IN THE LORD AND IN THE POWER OF HIS MIGHT" (see Ephesians 6:10).

When the devil caused me to feel fear—which is simply the evidence of his presence near us—I said boldly, *The Lord is my light and my salvation; whom shall I fear? The Lord is the strength of my life; of whom shall I be afraid? When the wicked, even mine enemies and my foes, came upon me to eat up my flesh, they stumbled and fell* (Psalm 27:1,2). PRAISE THE LORD!

Well, do you know what happened? I lived and got well! All fear and torment left me. I have flown all over this world many times and preached the Gospel.

Through this experience, the Lord taught me that Satan's attack is primarily in the mind. The thought life must be dominated by the Word of God. He allowed me to go through this to teach me, and to make it possible for me to teach you, the way to victory.

Use the Word

Since that time, I have stayed in my Bible. When the enemy tries to rush me with thoughts, I whip out the two-edged sword and face him squarely, just to let him know I am a victor through Jesus. I do this almost every day. With David of old, I climb up on the highest hill-top, as it were, and with my whole soul I confess Psalm 91 with a shout in the face of the devil and demonic forces:

"I dwell in the secret place of the most High. I abide under the shadow of the Almighty. I will say of the Lord—He is my refuge! He is my fortress! He is my God! In Him I trust. Surely He hath delivered ME from the snare of the fowler and from the noisome pestilence. He has covered me with His feathers and under His wings I trust.

"HIS TRUTH IS MY SHIELD AND BUCK-LER! Therefore, I am not afraid of the terror by night!

I am not afraid of the arrow that flieth by day! I am not afraid of the pestilence that walketh in darkness! I am not afraid of the destruction that wasteth at noonday. A thousand shall fall at my side and ten thousand at my right hand, but it shall not come nigh me. Only with mine eyes shall I behold and see the reward of the wicked. Because I have made the Lord, which is my refuge, even the most High, my habitation. No evil shall befall me, and NO PLAGUE SHALL COME NIGH MY DWELLING!" (See vss. 1-10.)

Why? Because He hath given His angels charge over John H. Osteen and all his household! He has charged His angels saying, "I charge you, angels, to keep him and his household, in ALL THEIR WAYS. Bear them up in your hands, lest they dash their feet against a stone!" (See vss. 11,12.)

Oh hallelujah! It is no wonder I can go on to say, "I tread upon the lion and the adder. The young lion and dragon I trample under my feet. Because I have set my love upon Him, He delivers me. He has set me on high because I have known His Name. I call upon Him and He answers me! HE IS WITH ME IN TROUBLE! He delivers me and honors me. With long life He satisfies me and shews me His salvation!" (See vss. 13-16.)

There is no room for the devil's thoughts when you fill your mind with thoughts like these from the Lord. I encourage you to pull your two-edged sword!

Wade into the battle fearlessly! Every Christian can whip the devil and drive out his devilish thoughts with "IT IS WRITTEN!"

Satan's thoughts

Remember, the battleground is in the mind. THOUGHTS are what Satan wants to put in your mind. You can see this throughout the Scriptures.

In Acts, chapter 8, we have the story of Philip going down to Samaria for a great revival. Many were saved, healed, delivered from the power of Satan, baptized in water, and baptized also in the Holy Spirit.

In this story, we see a man by the name of Simon, the sorcerer. In error, he offers Peter and John money for the gift of the laying on of hands to help people receive the Holy Spirit.

Peter rebuked him and said he was in the gall of bitterness and the bonds of iniquity. He said, "Pray that the THOUGHT OF THINE HEART may be forgiven thee." (See vs. 22.)

He was motivated by a THOUGHT! Where did that thought come from? It came from Satan!

Peter said, in effect, "Satan has put a thought in your heart. You have accepted it as your own and acted upon it. Now pray for God to forgive you for that THOUGHT!"

He did not say *thoughts* but *thought*. Pray that

12

God will forgive you for that ONE THOUGHT that leads you to wrong action.

Concerning the betrayal of Jesus, the Bible says, "The devil, having put into the heart of Judas to betray Him...." (See John 13:2.) Satan dropped the thought into the heart and mind of Judas.

You see, the enemy's primary approach is to drop a THOUGHT into our minds. He wants us to accept it and act upon it. *But those things which proceed out of the mouth come forth from the heart; and they defile the man. For out of the heart proceed EVIL THOUGHTS, murders, adulteries, fornications, thefts, false witness, blasphemies* (Matthew 15:18,19).

In Luke 24, Jesus appeared to His disciples after He had risen from the dead. The Bible says *they were terrified and affrighted* (vs. 37). Jesus chided them and said, *Why are ye troubled? and why do THOUGHTS arise in your hearts?* (vs. 38).

They were terrified. Where did this terror come from? It came from THOUGHTS they let into their hearts. These thoughts were allowed to arise and create tormenting FEAR.

Thousands of people who read this book are gripped by fear. That fear came from thoughts Satan put into their minds. They have accepted them and have lived in the torment they produce. CAST DOWN THOSE IMAGINATIONS! PULL DOWN THOSE

STRONGHOLDS! BRING EVERY THOUGHT INTO THE CAPTIVITY OF CHRIST!

Thoughts can become strongholds

A lying thought can become a STRONGHOLD. In other words, Satan's lying thoughts can have a strong hold on you—or hold you strongly.

I was in a distant city conducting some services. After one of the services, a young man about twenty years of age came to the platform to shake my hand. As soon as I took his hand, the Holy Ghost revealed to me that a homosexual devil had attacked him in his mind and was trying to get him to accept the THOUGHT that he was abnormal.

I said to him, "Young man, there is a homosexual devil after you. He has told you that you are abnormal." I looked into his eyes that were filled with the fear of this haunting thought and said, "You are not a homosexual. You are not abnormal. That thought came from Satan, and he is trying to get you to accept it and act upon it. God created you normal."

We rebuked the devil, cast out the thought, and he was free! I shall never forget the vanishing of the suffering I saw in his eyes.

This precious young man had been held captive by a devilish thought. He had received a THOUGHT from the enemy, and it had become a STRONGHOLD!

It held onto him with a strong hold. It produced IMAGINATIONS IN HIS MIND! He could imagine all the sorrows that would attend his life if he actually turned out to be abnormal. These imaginations produced FEAR! But thank God, HE PULLED DOWN THOSE STRONGHOLDS AND CAST DOWN THOSE IMAGINATIONS, and he was delivered from the lie of Satan.

Thoughts can hold you like a vise and keep you from the truth. One mighty lie from Satan, placed into your mind, can hold you in a place of sickness, suffering, and torment.

You ask, "How long?"

As long as you permit it. As long as you accept it.

Let me tell you a most amazing story that illustrates this point. I have a precious sister, Mary Givens. Many of you have read of her deliverance from a bed of affliction after the doctors had given her no hope of ever being well. But there is one facet of her deliverance and healing I have never written about. It has to do with the message of this book.

Mary's battle

I remember when Mary was saved. She was one of the first ones I had the privilege of winning to the Lord back in 1939. What a wonderful Christian she became. She faithfully served the Lord and was a blessing to hundreds of people in the Hampton Place Baptist Church in Dallas, Texas.

After many years of service for the Lord, she became very sick. (You can read her own testimony in my book *You Can Change Your Destiny*.) To briefly state it here does not adequately describe what she endured. She had violent attacks in her mind and body. She suffered untold agony for years. She was in and out of hospitals and institutions. They finally sent her home and said they could do no more for her. She was unable to walk. Her equilibrium was gone. She could not feed herself. She could not get up to go to the bathroom. At times, she screamed out in terror and begged to die. Satan was dragging her into deeper darkness, daily.

Finally, she could remember none of the scriptures she had memorized. She felt helpless in the grip of this satanic attack. And, at this time, she knew practically nothing about the Baptism in the Holy Spirit and healing by the power of Jesus' name. We had been taught that these things passed away with the apostles. Suffering, we were told, was from God and we were to patiently endure it.

My sister spent years in this state, finally coming to the place where she required nursing care twenty-four hours a day. When I finally saw her, she did not know me and I would not have recognized her on the streets of Dallas.

There she lay! What held her there on that bed? A THOUGHT! She was held captive by a thought the devil had put into her mind. He told her that her loving Heavenly Father was the One who sent this sickness and torment. He told her that she must suffer patiently and be faithful, for this was God's doing and she must not rebel against God.

WHAT A LIE! Yet this one thought was captivating her mind. It was a stronghold. And God said we are to PULL DOWN STRONGHOLDS!

When I was led by the Holy Ghost to go to Dallas and pray for her, I did not realize she had been through all this suffering nor did I know the extent of her illness. When I walked into that dark room and saw my sweet sister in that terrible state, I was shocked. I became angry. I said in a stern voice, "Don't tell me God did this to my sister!" That was the Holy Ghost speaking.

My sister did not know me, but I learned later that she heard those words and, down in her heart, said, "Well, maybe this sickness did not come from God."

This was the beginning of deliverance. SHE PULLED DOWN THAT STRONGHOLD! In her heart, she rejected the thought that Satan had placed in her mind.

Mary's victory

We stood over her bed and commanded the demons to leave her, the room, and the house, in the name of the LORD JESUS CHRIST. AND THEY DID!

She arose, and, in a matter of minutes, was healed, baptized in the Holy Ghost, and RAN—RAN through her home, praising God! SHE WAS DELIVERED THAT DAY! And that day she went to the table and fed herself!

She rejected a devilish THOUGHT that had her in captivity. She pulled down the stronghold.

To be sure, Satan tried to lie to her again and again in the next few weeks. He tried to place a thousand thoughts in her mind. But she refused to listen! She practiced bringing every thought into the captivity of Christ.

That happened many years ago, and she is still delivered and bringing deliverance to others.

No hope

Let me share another wonderful testimony. This is the story of one of God's precious handmaidens. She shared, "After eight years of suffering and five painful operations, a letter I received and a book I read caused me to decide it was time for a miracle."

This sister in the Lord described the horrors of those eight years of pain and misery with these sad words:

"January 1970, my doctor spoke the worst words

18

anyone could hear. He said, 'My child, you will have to go to bed and stay there and make it your life. You will probably be able to get up once or twice a day without too much pain, but that is only to go to the bathroom. I will prescribe pain killers for you.'

"I remember the month of March 1970 as being terrible. Not only was I on Darvon compound every four to six hours, but I was taking narcotics and a sleeping pill at night. On April 1, my body refused to accept any more medication!"

Now, look at the situation. Here was a Christian who was not only desperately ill but who was flooded with the thought that there was no remedy. The thought of the doctor's words, "There is no hope for you," lingered in her mind continually. This defeating thought and, I am sure, many others, flooded her heart and mind as she lay in that state of suffering. These thoughts became strongholds.

But the Lord made it possible for us to PULL DOWN STRONGHOLDS! And this suffering sister did just that. I have never read anything more thrilling than her account of how she daringly pulled down those strongholds of Satan by the Word of God!

Her first step toward deliverance was hearing the truth and replacing the devil's lie with the liberating truth of God's Word.

Messages from God

She tells of receiving a letter from her sister and how it lifted her faith and helped her believe for a miracle.

Then she tells of a young business woman who came to visit and pray for her. This woman left one of my books with her and, in the providence of God, it was the key to her finding help. She tells it like this:

"Before she left, she gave me a book by John H. Osteen, a Spirit-filled Baptist, entitled *You Can Change Your Destiny*. That morning, I read all the words of that book and re-read the first chapter six times! The third and fourth paragraphs of the first page stated:

> Have you become convinced that your destiny is to suffer pain and disease and defeat? Have you given up and resigned yourself to the position that there is nothing that can be done about your situation? You can change your destiny!

> Get out of your wheelchair, your bed. Open the doors, enlarge your coasts! I have seen multitudes change their destiny by believing these promises and rebelling against the devil. YOU WILL NEVER BE HEALED AS LONG AS YOU THINK GOD WANTS YOU TO BE SICK. It is the devil who wants you to suffer.

God wants you to be well. Rebel in your heart and be done with it. Faith is an act. To believe the Word is to act on the Word!

Do you see what happened when she read those words and the truth from God's Word presented in that book? She began to change her thinking and to replace her thoughts of "no hope" with the promises of God. She literally pulled down the strongholds of Satan by the Word of God!

It was not an easy task and she did not get well instantly...but she did get well! Praise be to the Lord! She stepped out in faith on God's Word and began to confess His promises. She began to act like God's thoughts were true.

Deliverance came

The battle raged on, but she did not give up. She refused the thoughts of sickness and defeat! She replaced them with the thoughts of God's promises to heal and deliver. And as she did, a change began to take place in her body. She sums up the complete healing like this:

"The doctor seemed more interested in my charts than in me. I asked him if he believed in miracles and he said, 'I most certainly do.' I said, 'Would you like to see a miracle walking?' He looked at me strangely and said, 'Well, yes.' Then I danced all over the room! He leaned against the examining table, visibly affected, saying, 'Tell me about it.' I told him and his eyes were full of tears when I finished."

Isn't that a wonderful testimony to the glory of Jesus? It was His promises that she relied on. It was the power of His Word that set her free! She pulled down the strongholds and today she is free from her suffering!

Satan's lies

Many of you who now read these words are held captive by a thought. And that thought brings fear. Here are some of the thoughts Satan drops into your mind: "You are no good." "You are a homosexual." "You are not saved." "You are not going to make heaven." "You are going to be lost forever." "Your children are going to hell." "You are going to have a wreck." "No one appreciates you." "Your wife doesn't love you any more." "Your husband doesn't love you any more." "You have cancer." "You have a tumor of the brain." "You will never get well." "You would be better off dead." "It's just as bad to think a thing as to do it, so go ahead and do it."

The thoughts go on and on. The devil introduces thousands of lies to your mind. When you accept them as your own thoughts, you begin to say with your mouth what Satan has said to your mind.

I hear people doing this all the time. They hear the

thought, it brings fear, and then they begin to SAY what Satan has planted in their mind. They speak the thoughts: "I am no good." "I am abnormal." "I am not saved." "I'll never make heaven." "I am lost!" "My children will never get saved." "I am going to have a wreck." "No one appreciates me." "My mate doesn't love me any more."

They verbalize the thoughts, signifying that they have accepted them. The lie causes them to say, in fear, "I have cancer." "I have a brain tumor." "I will never get well." "I'd be better off dead." "It is just as bad to think a thing as to do it, so I might as well go ahead and give myself over to this sin."

Does some thought hold you strongly today? Be aware of the tricks of the enemy. The Bible says, "We are not ignorant of his devices" (see 2 Corinthians 2:11). So don't fall into his trap. The Bible says, "Bring every thought into the captivity of Christ."

Imaginations bring fear

One night, as I lay in bed waiting for our son to return home, I was bombarded with bad thoughts. They came thick and fast. "He has had a bad wreck." "He will never make it home." "You have seen him alive for the last time." On and on they came. Without realizing it, I let these thoughts linger, and I began to have IMAGINATIONS. I could see him in that wreck. I could see

23

the ambulance hurrying to get him. I could see him bleeding. Fear hit the pit of my stomach.

Suddenly I caught on to what was happening. I was listening to the thoughts of the enemy. He wanted to torment me. I began to quote the Word of God! I told the devil what God had said about me and my household. I told him the promises God had made to me. I rebuked the bad thoughts and replaced them with the WORD OF GOD. I began to say what God had promised in His Word.

The fear left, and peace, like a gentle dove, came into my heart. I was so happy! As I rearranged my pillow to enjoy a good night's sleep, I heard the front door open. It was my son, safe and sound. Praise the Lord!

When you repeat out loud the lies Satan puts in your thoughts, you become fearful and live in torment. But when you accept God's thoughts and promises and repeat them out loud in faith, they bring peace to your heart.

The Bible is full of God's thoughts. Replace every thought the devil tries to force on you with one of God's thoughts.

Overcome the devil with God's Word

Remember, the devil is a liar and the father of all lies. He cannot tell the truth. If you will take just the opposite of what the devil has told you, then you will know the truth!

The way we practice this in our home is this: When the devil comes along with a thought to create fear, we say, "Why, thank you so much, Mr. Devil, for telling me that. Now I know the truth! I'll just take the opposite of what you say and know the truth about the situation." Then we replace that thought with a scripture to back it up!

Now, let me encourage you. If the devil says you are not saved, replace that thought with the scripture, *As many as received him, to them gave he power to become the sons of God, even to them that believe on his name* (John 1:12). Confess that boldly and the lie will leave.

If the devil says you are going to die early in life and leave your family, shout loudly what David said in Psalm 91, "With long life he satisfies me and shows me His salvation!" (see vs. 16).

If the devil says you will never get well, cry out joyfully, "With His stripes I am healed!" (see Isaiah 53:5).

If the enemy tells you God will not forgive your sin or heal your particular disease, replace that thought with one of God's precious healing, delivering thoughts: "Bless the Lord, O my soul: and all that is within me, bless his holy name. Bless the Lord, O my soul, and forget not all his benefits: WHO FORGIVETH ALL

MINE INIQUITIES, WHO HEALETH ALL MY DISEASES" (see Psalm 103:1-3).

If the thought comes that you are rejected and destitute, replace it with the scripture, *He will regard the prayer of the destitute* (Psalm 102:17).

If the devil drops the thought into your mind that you are a homosexual, don't let fear grip you. Replace that thought with God's Word. Say, "Satan, the Bible says that *if any man be in Christ, he is a new creature: old things are passed away; behold, all things are become new* (2 Corinthians 5:17). I am a NEW creature in Christ! I am more than a conqueror! *Greater is he* [Jesus] *that is in* [me], *than he that is in the world* (1 John 4:4). I rebuke you, you lying demon! In the name of Jesus Christ, I cast you and your thoughts out of my mind. Go, in Jesus' name!"

He will go...the thoughts will go...and fear will go! You will smile and stand up tall for Jesus!

Your Father in heaven will say about you what He said about Job. "Have you seen my servant? There is none like him!" (See Job 1:8.)

I could go on and on, but you can apply this to your own situation.

This is the plan Jesus used when He whipped the devil. Satan placed the thought in His mind, "Turn these stones to bread." Jesus rejected that thought and replaced it with one of God's thoughts by saying, "IT IS

WRITTEN." (See Matthew 4:1-10.)

You, too, can whip the devil every time by saying, "It is written!" Then, go on to say what is written in the promises of God.

BRING EVERY THOUGHT INTO THE CAP-TIVITY OF CHRIST! That means, bring every thought under the dominion of the Word of God. Make the devil's thoughts bow to the infallible Word of God. Drive them out with the promises of God. Pull them down with, "THUS SAITH THE LORD!"

Isaiah 54:17 tells us, *No WEAPON that is formed against thee shall prosper; and every TONGUE that shall rise against thee in judgment thou shalt condemn. This is the heritage of the servants of the Lord, and their righteousness is of me, saith the Lord.*

What weapon? What tongue? A thought from Satan is a weapon, as is an accusation by an enemy. And this scripture says no weapon or tongue formed against you can prosper—unless you let it!

Many suffering, tormented people cry out to God to help them. But He has said, *Every tongue that shall rise up against you...thou*—THOU—*shalt condemn.* In other words, YOU are the one who is to condemn that tongue. YOU are the one who is to condemn that thought. YOU are the one who shall rebuke Satan and his lies!

Don't ask God to do it! Don't expect Jesus to do

it! HE TOLD *YOU* TO DO IT!

Every tongue or thought that rises against you to bring condemnation, fear, torment, and defeat, shall be condemned and cast down and out by YOU. He said, "THOU SHALT CONDEMN!"

Jesus conquered Satan for you, then gave you His authority to demonstrate the devil's defeat. *Behold, I give unto YOU power...over all the power of the enemy* (Luke 10:19). "In my name YOU shall cast out devils" (see Mark 16:17).

Renew your mind

The thought life is the battlefield. So guard your thoughts. Watch what you read. Watch what you look at. Watch what you let into your mind. Do not let wrong thoughts linger there.

I beseech you therefore, brethren, by the mercies of God, that ye present your bodies a living sacrifice, holy, acceptable unto God, which is your reasonable service. And be not conformed to this world: but be ye transformed by the renewing of your mind, that ye may prove what is that good, and acceptable, and perfect, will of God (Romans 12:1,2).

How are we transformed? By the RENEWING OF OUR MINDS! Live in the Word. Walk daily with Abraham, Isaac, Jacob, Isaiah, Jeremiah, Ezekiel, Peter, Paul, and the others. Take the hand of Jesus and walk with Him through Matthew, Mark, Luke, and John. Think God's thoughts daily! Renew your mind. Learn to think like God thinks about salvation, forgiveness, mercy, sickness, healing, deliverance, love, goodness, and all the other wonderful things in the Bible.

David said he was blessed. Why? Listen to him in Psalm 1: *BLESSED is the man that walketh not in the counsel of the ungodly, nor standeth in the way of sinners, nor sitteth in the seat of the scornful. But his delight is in the law of the Lord; and in his law doth he meditate day and night. And he shall be like a tree planted by the rivers of water, that bringeth forth his fruit in his season; his leaf also shall not wither; and whatsoever he doeth shall prosper* (vss. 1-3).

Notice, he says, *His DELIGHT is in the law of the Lord...and in His law he MEDITATES.* Then he tells us *when* he meditates: He meditates in the Word of God DAY AND NIGHT.

The man who delights and meditates in the law of the Lord is a man who can pull down strongholds and cast down imaginations!

Consider our key scripture again: *For the weapons of our warfare are not carnal, but mighty through God to the pulling down of strong holds; casting down imaginations, and every high thing that exalteth itself against the knowledge of God, and bringing into captivity every thought to the obedience of Christ* (2 Corinthians 10:4,5).

This speaks of THOUGHTS. These thoughts are STRONGHOLDS. They produce IMAGINATIONS. Then come fear, torment, sickness, and defeat!

The battlefield is the THOUGHT LIFE. But, our loving Father has provided us with divine ammunition. He said, "Our weapons are not carnal, but mighty through God to the pulling down of strongholds and casting down of imaginations and bringing every thought into the captivity of Christ." Thank God, now you have learned to replace lying thoughts with God's thoughts from the promises in the Bible. Now you can pull down those strongholds and cast down those imaginations that have defeated you.

You don't play with them or deal with them lightly. You refuse to allow them to linger. YOU PULL THEM DOWN AND CAST THEM OUT!

It's up to YOU

Now you know that God has given you the power to pull down strongholds and He expects YOU to do it. Christ died that you might have that authority, and He expects you to use it. AND SO YOU WILL!

This is a WARFARE! But we *do* have WEAPONS. And our weapons are not carnal..our weapons are not of the flesh. The Bible says THEY ARE MIGHTY THROUGH GOD! God has provided you with mighty weapons so you can win this warfare in the thought life.

He has given you HIS WORD, THE BLOOD OF JESUS, and THE NAME OF JESUS!

Remember, you are not alone. When you dare to do your part, all heaven comes to your aid. YOU rise up and do battle. YOU pull down those strongholds. YOU cast down those imaginations. YOU condemn every tongue or thought that rises against you. YOU refuse to allow negative, destructive, devilish thoughts to linger in your mind to meditate on them.

I know of homes that were blasted asunder by divorce, all because Satan placed a lying thought into the mind of one of the mates. That person allowed that thought to linger and meditated on it until it became an obsession with them. They believed it so strongly that they felt justified in any action they decided to take. That thought was a STRONGHOLD!

When one continual thought lingers and becomes a stronghold, it allows others, similar to it, to also dominate the thinking. This leads to action and all the misery and heartache that inevitably follow.

I am compelled to share this message because this is a day when the legions of wickedness have been loosed upon the Body of Christ. Mothers, fathers, ministers, missionaries, young men and women—all are feeling the effects of this satanic attack. Ministries are being destroyed. Young people are drowning in the cesspool of drugs. Homes are being assaulted and wrecked. Not only this, but multiplied thousands of God's precious people are living in mental and spiritual torment. Innumerable Christians are, this very day, suffering pain, disease, and physical maladies. They have prayed and sought the way out but to no avail.

There are no *easy* answers. But my message to you today is...THERE IS AN ANSWER!

If you will resolve to follow God's commands, as outlined in this book, and rise up with the Word of God and RENEW YOUR MIND, God will lift you out of that horrible pit and set your feet upon the solid rock. He will put a new song in your heart—even praise unto your God.

Seed thoughts

You create the atmosphere in which you live by the thoughts you entertain for constant meditation. Thoughts are like the seeds in trees and flowers. When they are planted, they will "bring forth after their kind" (see Genesis 1:11,12). God said in Isaiah 57:19, *I create the fruit of the lips.*

I am not talking about "mind over matter." That is foolishness. I am speaking of filling our minds with the mighty creative thoughts found in the Word of Almighty God.

Take a man who "thinks poverty," place him in the richest surroundings, and give him good opportunities and, eventually, he will change his surroundings by his "seed thoughts" of poverty. He will become poor again. His thoughts, like seeds, will create the atmosphere around him.

Likewise, a man filled with God's great thoughts of prosperity will create that atmosphere wherever he goes. Even if you place him in the most poverty-stricken surroundings, the seed thoughts of prosperity will drive out the poverty thoughts and fill the atmosphere around him with success. He will become prosperous again.

You CAN determine the atmosphere in which you live by the seed thoughts you plant in your mind of the great, unchanging promises of God. You can literally change your atmosphere by changing your thoughts and the words you speak.

You cannot sow seed thoughts of sickness and live in an atmosphere of health. You cannot sow seed thoughts of defeat and fear and live in an atmosphere of victory and peace. You cannot sow seed thoughts of poverty and live in an atmosphere of prosperity.

Begin, today, to fill your mind, mouth, heart, home, and surroundings with the marvelous, loving seed thoughts of God about health, victory, peace, prosperity, and all the other things you desire in life. Base these thoughts on *definite* promises of God. Think them...talk them...act on them!

This is what the Lord meant when He stated, "As

a man thinketh in his heart, so is he" (see Proverbs 23:7).

Now you know the truth! The rest is up to you!

I visualize faith rising in your heart. It seems that I can see this mighty revelation dawning in your soul. You are determined that you will not be denied. You have found the reason for defeat. You have found the way to change things. You have seen the pathway to victory!

Arise, precious child of God, and enter into the joy of thy Lord!

BOOKS BY JOHN OSTEEN

*A Miracle For Your Marriage
*A Place Called There
*ABC's of Faith
*Believing God For Your Loved Ones
 Deception! Recognizing True and False Ministries
 Four Principles in Receiving From God
*Healed of Cancer by Dodie Osteen
*How To Claim the Benefits of the Will
*How To Demonstrate Satan's Defeat
 How To Flow in the Super Supernatural
 How To Minister Healing to the Sick
*How To Receive Life Eternal
 How To Release the Power of God
 Keep What God Gives
*Love & Marriage
 Overcoming Hindrances To Receiving the Baptism in the Holy Spirit
*Overcoming Opposition: How To Succeed in Doing the Will of God
    by Lisa Comes
*Pulling Down Strongholds
*Receive the Holy Spirit
 Reigning in Life as a King
 Rivers of Living Water
 Saturday's Coming
 Seven Facts About Prevailing Prayer
 Seven Qualities of a Man of Faith
*Six Lies the Devil Uses To Destroy Marriages by Lisa Comes
 Spiritual Food For Victorious Living
*The Believer's #1 Need
 The Bible Way to Spiritual Power
 The Confessions of a Baptist Preacher
*The Divine Flow
*The 6th Sense...Faith
 The Truth Shall Set You Free
*There Is a Miracle in Your Mouth
 This Awakening Generation
 Unraveling the Mystery of the Blood Covenant
*What To Do When Nothing Seems To Work
*What To Do When the Tempter Comes
 You Can Change Your Destiny

*Also available in Spanish.

Please write for a complete list of prices in the John Osteen Library.
Lakewood Church • P.O. Box 23297 • Houston, Texas 77228